THE TOTALLY GRUESOME HORROR COLORING BOOK

THE TOTALLY GRUESOME HORROR COLORING BOOK

JUAN CALLE AND SANTIAGO CALLE

SIRIUS

SIRIUS

This edition published in 2024 by Sirius Publishing, a division of
Arcturus Publishing Limited,
26/27 Bickels Yard, 151–153 Bermondsey Street,
London SE1 3HA

ISBN: 978-1-3988-4342-4
CH011538NT

Printed in China

INTRODUCTION

A whole world of horror awaits you in the more than 100 images in this truly terrifying coloring book. You will find skulls with spider legs that suck out your eyeballs as you sleep, a beautifully dressed Victorian trio revealing their zombie predilections with crazed eyes and spiky teeth, and a heart worn outside the body, and a modern-day Frankenstein's monster with part of his skull removed so you can see the inner workings of the brain. The horror scenarios range from the depths of the ocean to the furthest wastes of space, and back in time to gruesome incidents in history.

Gather a selection of colored pencils or markers in a suitably gory palette, find a space where no-one can hear you scream, and begin to color your own gruesome artwork.

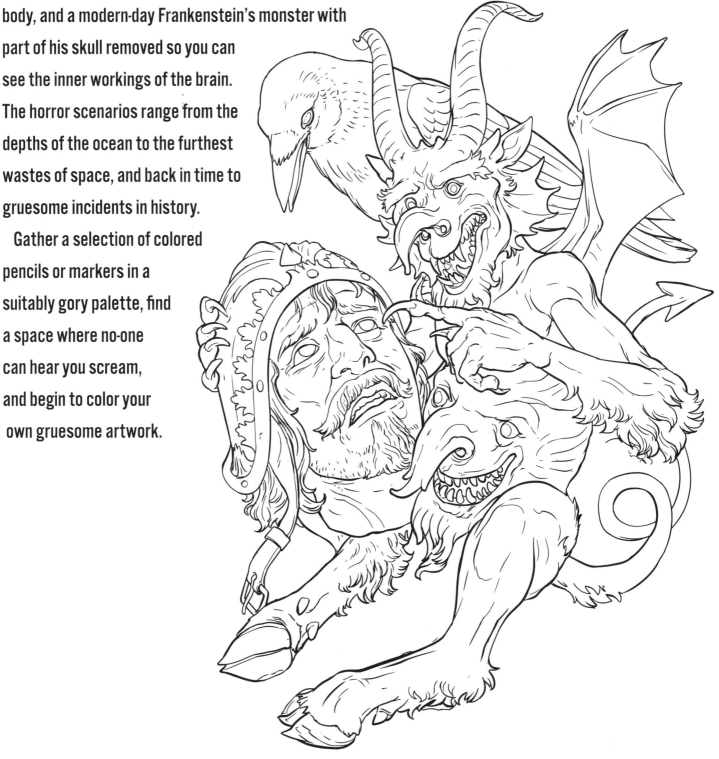

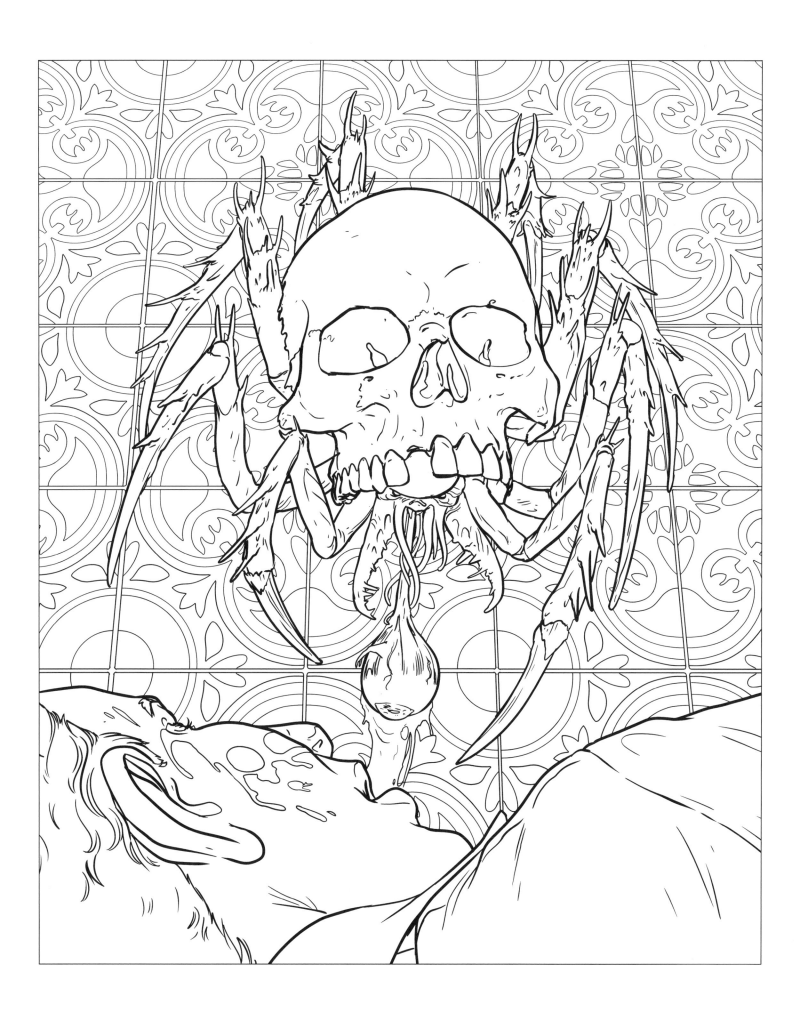

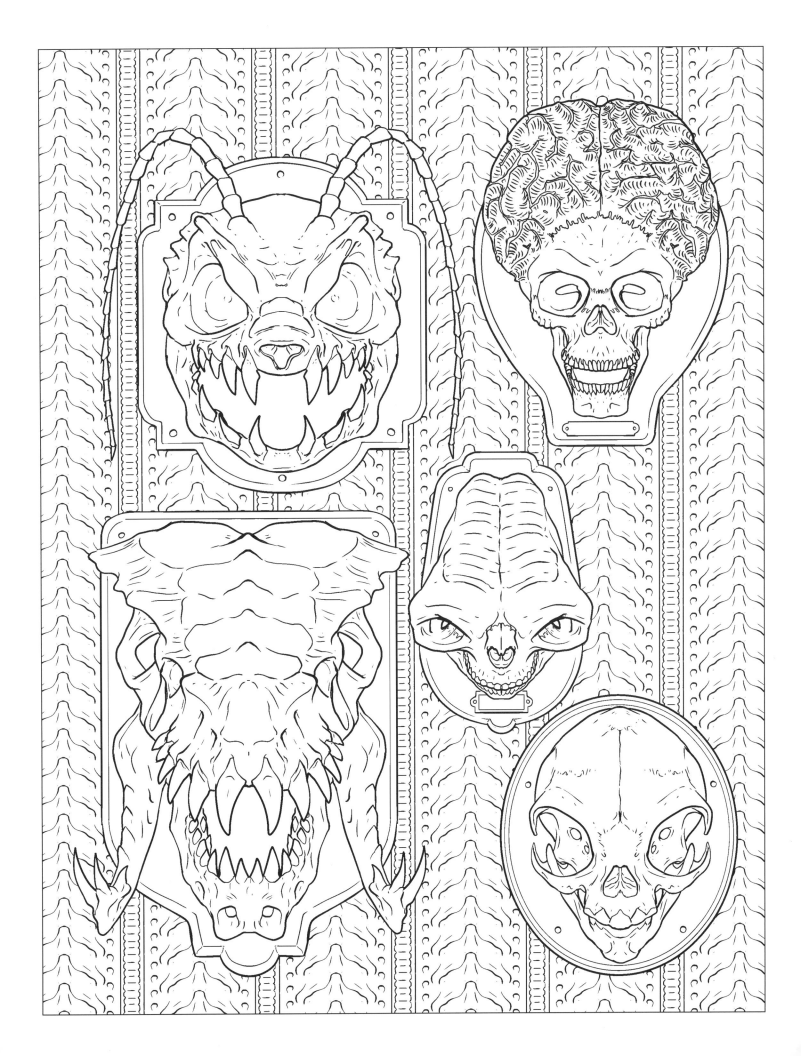

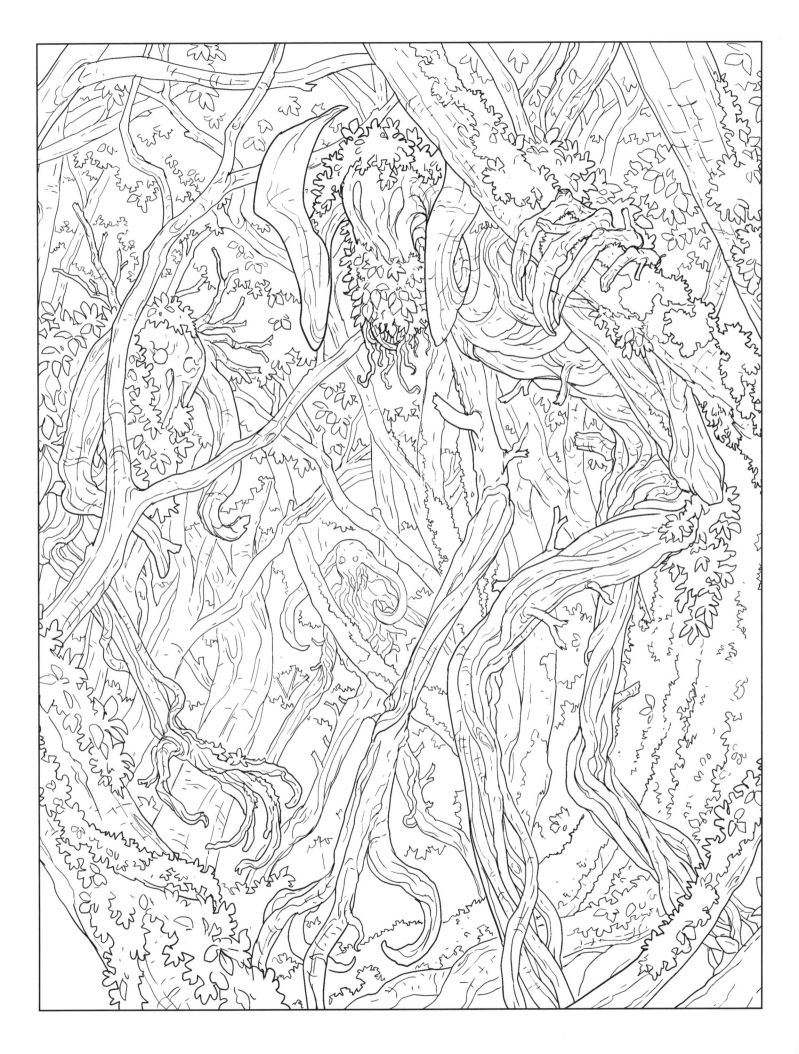

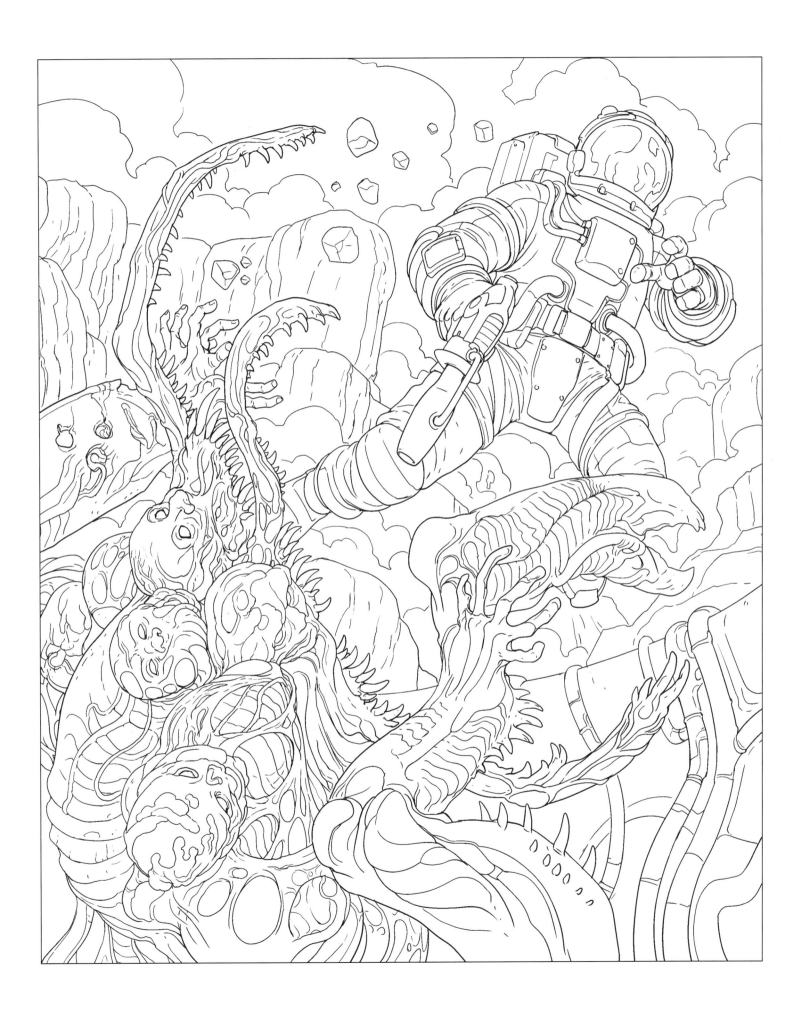

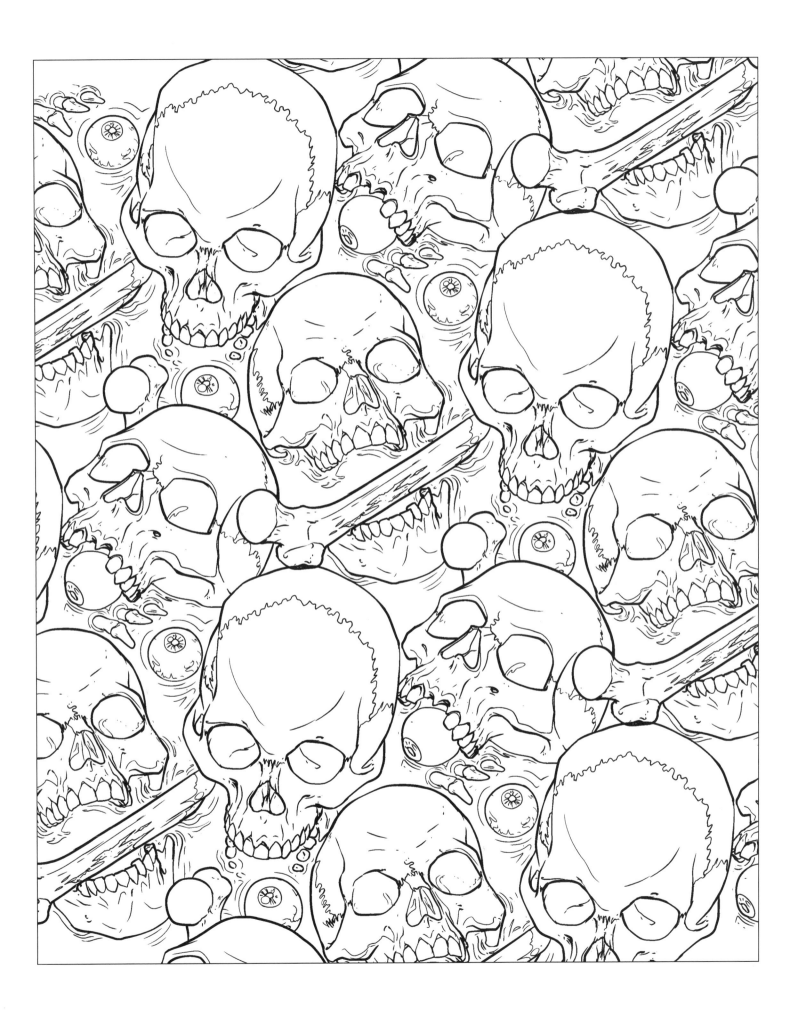

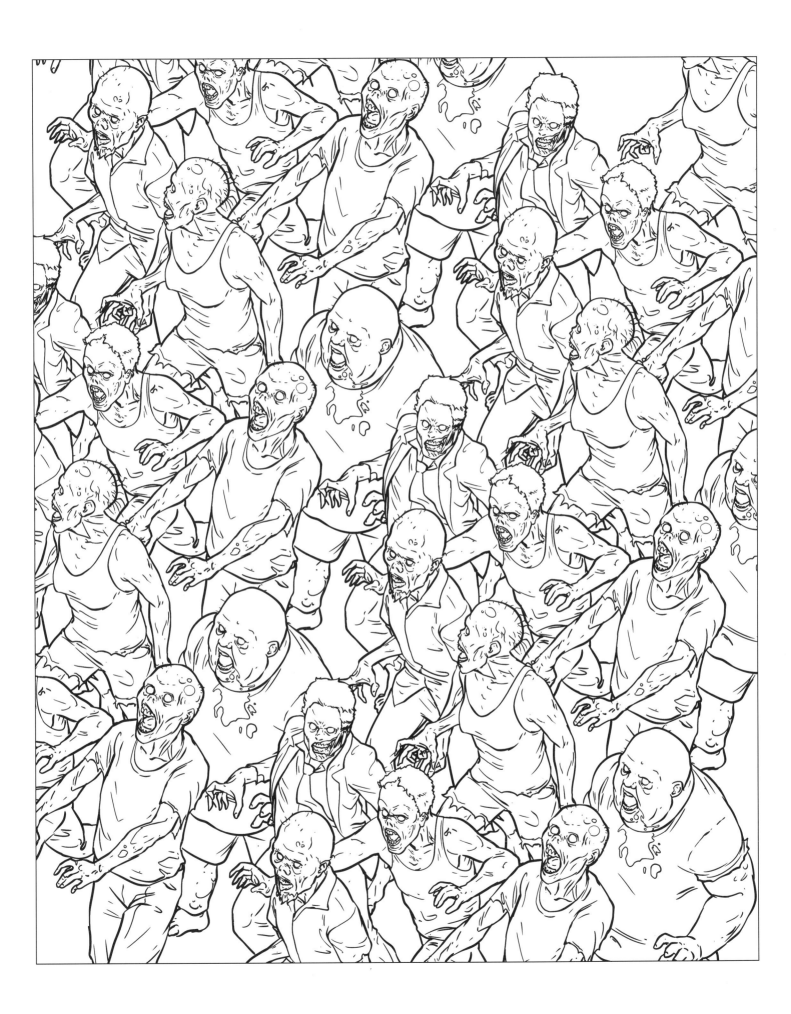

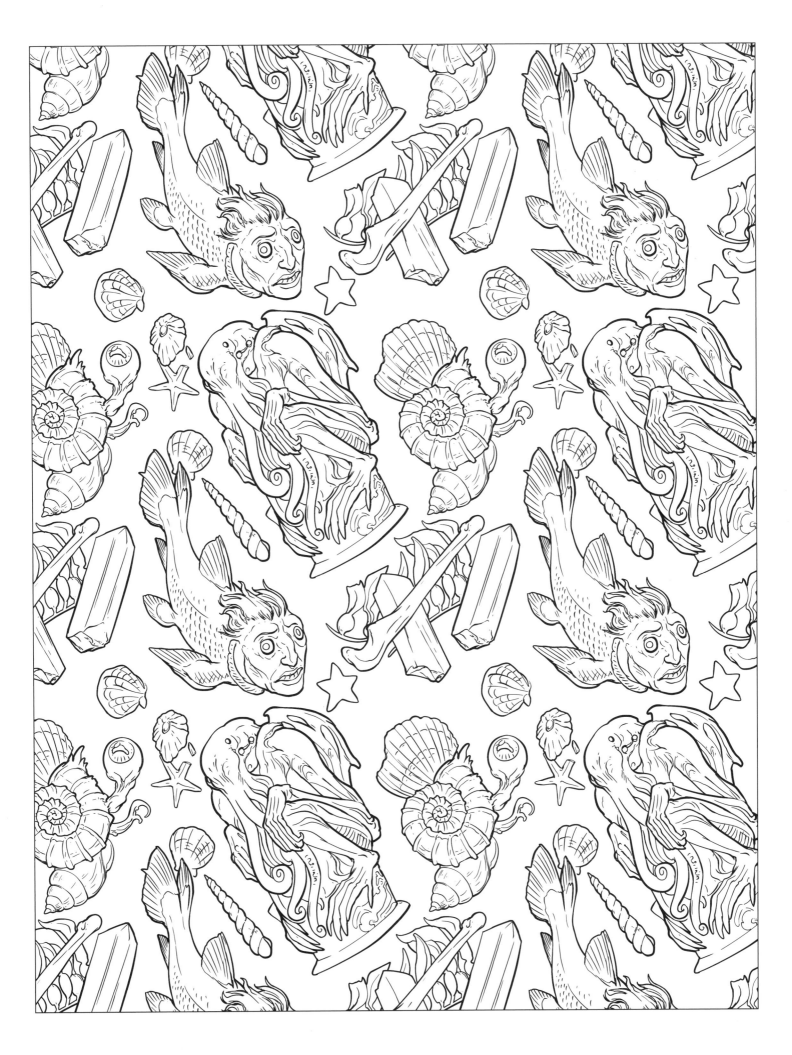

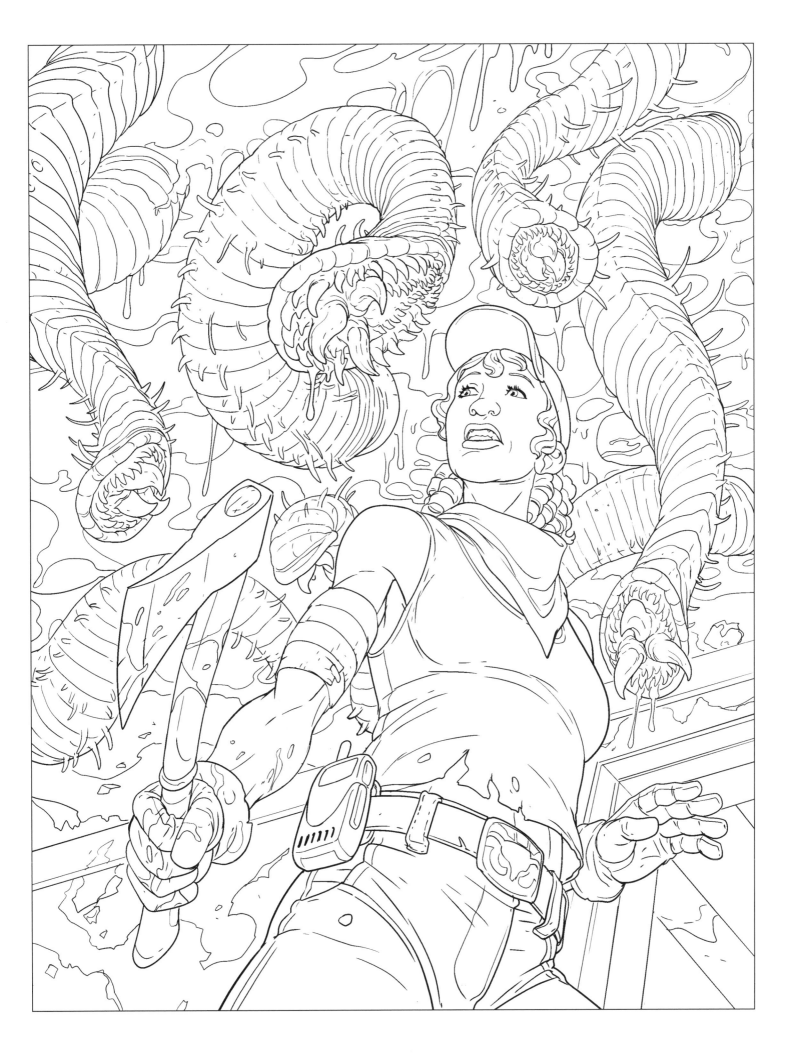

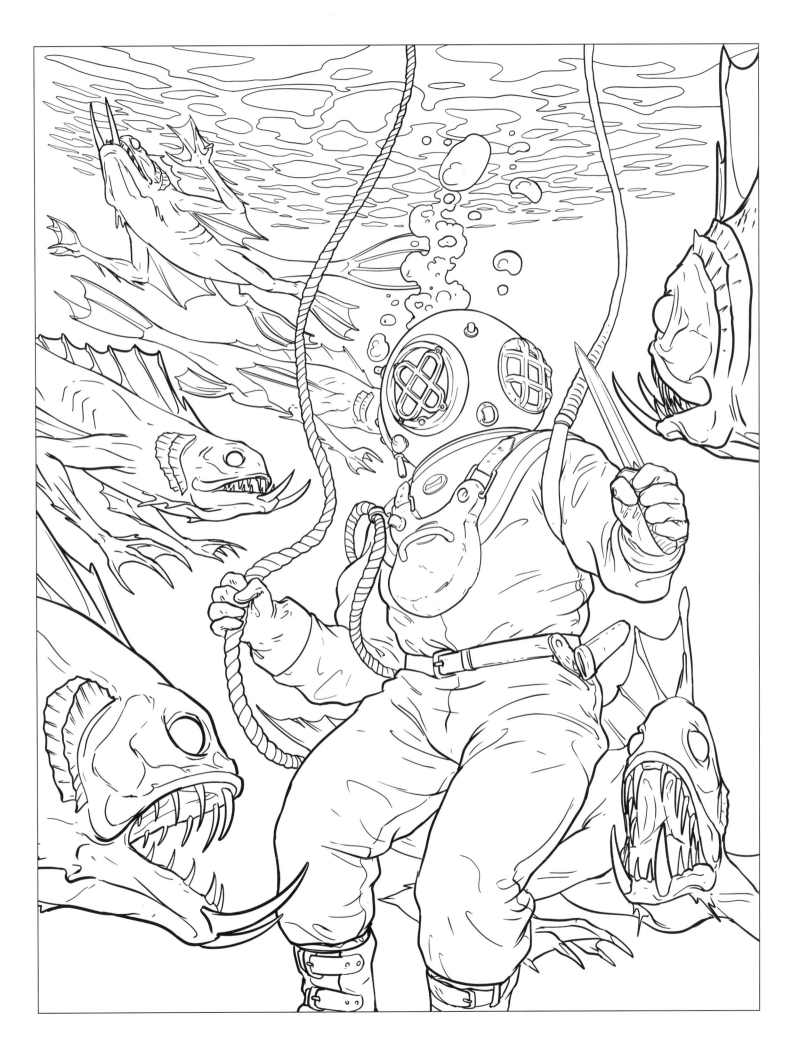